BUYING AMAZON RETURN PALLETS

Simple Ways to Earn Money Using
Amazon's Liquidation Pallets

INTRODUCTION

Online shopping is quickly becoming the standard, and Amazon, the largest online marketplace, has seen the greatest influx of customers. However, Amazon's exceptional expansion has resulted in an increase in the number of returns.

So, if you want to sell on Amazon, you should be ready to get product returns from time to time. While this may not be entirely due to the quality of your goods, it has a direct impact on your return rate, and a high return rate may result in your Amazon account being suspended.

Returns are bad for sellers in the long term, but they can be a boon for resellers who understand how to acquire Amazon return pallets.

In this book, I'll show you how to buy Amazon return pallets, where to buy them, and how to resell them for a profit. But first, let's look at some Amazon return statistics to understand why people return Amazon purchases.

Chapter 1

Why do Amazon customers return products?

According to statistics, around 67% of online shoppers review the returns page prior to placing a purchase. As a result, it is not unexpected that Amazon's accommodating return policy is one of the primary reasons why consumers like to shop there.

People, on the other hand, do not shop online with the intention of returning their purchases. Although some reasons for product returns are intangible, most customers return things because they are damaged, defective, of poor quality, or, in certain circumstances, they did not receive what they expected.

20% of customers returned things because they were damaged, 21% received a product that appeared different from what was ordered, 23% received the incorrect item, and 36 percent returned products for reasons best known to them.

The reasons for returns may be understandable from the customer's perspective, but too many returns might be detrimental to Amazon merchants. Thankfully, retailers can now purchase Amazon return pallets, resell them, and make a profit rather than incurring total losses.

Chapter 2

What Happens to Product Returns on Amazon?

Depending on the state of the returned goods, Amazon has multiple options for managing returned merchandise.

They often resell things in good shape and discard those that are damaged. They do, however, liquidate in some situations. Amazon merely distributes the returned goods to partner companies that specialize in reselling returned goods when they liquidate.

Amazon return pallets are frequently used for liquidation.

Amazon announced the launch of liquidation resale sites in 2021 to assist sellers in reselling returned merchandise.

For FBA sellers who want to relist and resell their returned inventory on Amazon as used products, there is the Grade and Resell program. There's also Amazon Outlet, a program that allows retailers to sell overstocked products. Amazon also operates a daily deals website called Woot, which is a terrific spot for merchants to resale their products.

These channels may sound or perform well, but not all sellers want to deal with the stress of receiving returned items, repacking them, and then relisting them on Amazon. Sellers who prefer not to deal with this tension can instead discover how to purchase Amazon liquidation pallets.

Chapter 3

What exactly are Amazon Return Pallets?

Amazon Return Pallets are big wooden pallets used to ship merchandise back to Amazon. They are almost the same size as a standard pallet and include openings in the top and bottom to facilitate loading and unloading from a truck.

Third-party vendors who sell products on Amazon

frequently use Amazon Return Pallets. When these vendors receive an order from Amazon, they will ship the merchandise in an Amazon Return Pallet to the purchaser. If the goods are broken or defective, the seller can return them to Amazon using the return pallet.

Amazon also arranges client returns into distinct boxes and then sells them at a discount to large corporations. These companies then sell the goods to resellers who are willing to accept the risk.

How Amazon Free Return Policy Works

To comprehend what Amazon $1 pallets are for sale, you must first grasp the free return policy offered by large retail platforms such as Amazon. When things are damaged or unsatisfactory, the free return policy allows customers to be more flexible in their purchasing decisions. However, the number of returned Amazon pallets and merchandise is increasing.

These returned items cannot simply sit on the return shelf; they must be sold. When products are returned, they are inspected and resoldability is determined. Amazon ensures that the returned products are sold to other consumers in this manner.

The expense of reopening the return pallets, inspecting, stocking, and repacking, on the other hand, is very high. As a result, vendors that have their products returned frequently keep them as Amazon return pallets. Amazon return pallets are goods that have already been boxed and sent for Amazon pallet sales but have been returned to Amazon in pallets. Amazon can then sell these to businesses that are looking to purchase return pallets. Purchasing unopened return pallets from other Amazon merchants poses no risk. This is due to the fact that the pallets have been in transit multiple times and the products have not been checked.

The product may be somewhat damaged or not in their original state. However, the products are frequently undamaged and have suffered little or no damage during transit. Because the return pallet is not opened and checked, the pallet is equivalent to an Amazon mystery pallet for the new merchant. The discounted rates at which the shipments are sold provide a benefit to vendors who purchase these unseen packages. The vendor that purchases return pallets is not required to source or manufacture his goods. He can purchase these return pallets and resell new and reconditioned merchandise.

Fortunately, there is currently a high need for reconditioned and refurbished items. People are looking to buy these things from Internet stores.

Chapter 4

Buying Amazon Return Pallets

Amazon frequently creates return pallets to facilitate quick and easy liquidation. As a result, they generally sell to liquidators who can accept huge quantities of inventory at once. These liquidators then sell the returned pallets at a low cost to resellers and small enterprises.

So, rather than going via middlemen who would most certainly inflate the price, you can acquire Amazon returns from liquidation firms. These companies acquire return pallets at Amazon liquidation auctions.

Amazon Liquidation Sales

Bids are used by liquidation companies to purchase return pallets from Amazon. Registered liquidation firms can easily submit bids and get a truckload of overstocked returned goods or inventory. The Amazon liquidation auction is an excellent choice for large corporate purchasers looking, to begin with a diverse inventory.

The sole stipulation is that Amazon does not reveal the contents of the pallets, and these companies do not reveal the contents of the pallets to resellers.

What Should an Amazon Return Pallet Include?

A return pallet's contents are entirely unpredictable. Pallets are often filled with a variety of merchandise from several categories. As an example, one pallet could contain gadgets, clothing, beauty products, video games, and other items.

Some liquidation websites include a few photographs, which are usually insufficient because you can't view the complete pallet. Some liquidation websites, on the other hand, provide a manifest consisting of a number of pages that lists every item in the pallet, so you can view everything it contains.

The only disadvantage of purchasing Amazon returns is that not all of the things will be in excellent condition. Some may be unsuited for sale, while others may be excellent for resale. Some may require you to repair or touch up before reselling.

Is it better to buy Amazon returns or liquidation pallets?

Consider all of your options before purchasing Amazon returns. While purchasing Amazon pallets may be a fantastic idea if you plan to start a retail arbitrage business, you should proceed with caution or you may end up losing more money than you intended for.

Yes, you can buy a broad variety of things at a great

discount, but if the majority of them are unsellable, you may wind up losing money. So, while purchasing Amazon pallets has advantages, it also has disadvantages that should not be overlooked.

The following are some advantages and disadvantages of purchasing return pallets:

Benefits

- **You can buy in modest quantities and save money.**

Purchasing Amazon return pallets is an excellent strategy to reduce your startup costs for your resale business. You get to buy a large amount of stuff at a low cost.

- **You need not need a massive warehouse.**

Because you will be purchasing items in pieces, you will not require much storage, which is a gain because you will save money on storage.

- **You can avoid the intermediaries.**

Purchasing return pallets saves you more money than purchasing from wholesalers or middlemen who charge a markup.

Drawbacks

- You will not be given a detailed description of what is contained within the pallet. This can be dangerous, especially if you prefer to sell in a single category.

- If you get broken goods, you may end up with unsalable inventory.
- If you intend to expand your Amazon business, this business strategy is highly unsustainable and may not work for you in the long run.

Chapter 5

Where Can I Purchase Amazon Return Pallets?

Amazon return pallets can be purchased from liquidation companies. There are numerous liquidation companies to pick from, but you must ensure that you are purchasing from reputable organizations. Here are some liquidation companies where you can buy Amazon returns.

Liquidation.com

Liquidation.com is one of the largest and most trustworthy liquidation firms. Most resellers who acquire Amazon returns first look on this website.

Liquidation.com sells Amazon return pallets through auctions, so you must register and bid. However, Liquidation.com, like most liquidation companies, does not disclose any information regarding the contents of the return pallets, so retailers will have to find out for themselves after purchasing.

Direct Liquidation

Direct Liquidation is comparable to liquidation.com in that both companies work with huge stores such as Amazon, Target, and Walmart. As a result, you may expect to find fantastic offers on this website.

Direct liquidation.com allows you to refine your search by the marketplace. If you only want to buy Amazon customer returns, you can search for and discover Amazon pallet alternatives.

Direct liquidation does not provide thorough descriptions of the contents of their pallets, however, they do occasionally attach photographs. However, don't rely on the photos because they rarely really represent the content of the pallet.

This website, like liquidation.com, exclusively sells pallets by auction, so you must sign up and submit bids to get a pallet of interest.

888Lots.com

888Lots.com is not as well-known as the others mentioned before. They get the majority of their pallets from Amazon, and the best part about buying Amazon returns from 888lots.com is that you can get specific products at drastically reduced costs.

They also include a manifest, which is a thorough description of the contents of their pallets, as well as an Amazon calculator to assist you estimate your costs and determine whether the pallet is a good bargain.

While you may be able to purchase particular products at incredibly low costs, you may not always receive the best offers because goods may be defective.

888 Lots demands a current resale certificate from US customers. If you are not based in the United States, you must produce a valid business registration paperwork.

Bulq

Bulq is another popular liquidation company that buys consumer returns in bulk from several online marketplaces other than Amazon.

Bulq, unlike the bulk of other liquidation companies, does not sell by auction. When you see a pallet you want, all you have to do is add it to your cart and pay for it.

They provide a full description and photographs of your pallet, but you cannot be certain of the content of your pallet or the quality of the merchandise.

BlueLots

Bluelots is another well-known liquidation company that allows resellers to easily purchase Amazon refunds or customer returns from other marketplaces.

They have a search option that allows you to find pallets from any marketplace you choose, which is useful because they frequently have a mix of pallets from multiple marketplaces.

BlueLots delivers a variety of return-pallet information, allowing you to make an informed decision. You can view full manifests and clear images to get a sense of the pallet's contents.

Chapter 6

How Much Does Amazon Return Pallets Cost?

The price of an Amazon liquidation pallet varies depending on the size of the pallet and the liquidation website from which you wish to purchase. Some liquidation websites have fixed fees, whilst others hold auctions and sell based on bids.

Rates per pallet might range from $100 to $5,000 on average, depending on the quality and value of the commodities. This pricing range, however, may not apply to all pallets or websites, as some pallets might cost as much as $10,000.

Shipment rates vary amongst liquidation companies, while some provide free shipment.

Typically, you will be responsible for the shipping charges, which are decided by the size of your item and the distance between the delivery destination and your location.

Chapter 7

Pro Tips for Buying Amazon Return Pallets

Before you decide to buy Amazon returns, do your research and arm yourself with enough information to assure you get your money back. We'll assist you get valuable return pallets now that you have a list of places to buy return pallets from.

Find Out More About the Liquidation Company

Don't just start sourcing return pallets from any website; instead, take the time to learn more about the companies. People who have previously purchased from them may have useful information, such as the best categories to buy, the customer experience, and so on.

Checking through online reviews is an excellent approach to learn more about a liquidation company. You can make better informed bidding decisions if you know as much as possible about the item, the business, the quality of the goods, and the return policies.

Examine the Purchase Conditions

Before placing a bid, be sure you understand the condition of the merchandise. Also, keep in mind that some items may require refurbishment, so make sure you have the time to do so. If the website from which you're purchasing offers a manifest, read it carefully and try to understand the item descriptions, number, and estimated worth.

Obtain an Estimate of Your Shipping Costs

When it comes to reselling, your shipping expenses are the most important predictor of your net profit. So, before you make a purchase, receive an accurate estimate of the delivery charges. You may end yourself spending more on delivery than you did on the actual transaction.

Before you bid on a pallet, make sure the delivery cost is worthwhile.

Be Selective

If this is your first time buying pallets, ask around for recommendations. It is not suggested to purchase a pallet of electronics for the first time because they may be difficult to repair, resulting in a loss in the long term.

In addition, compare liquidation websites and choose the ones with the greatest pricing. Remember, the goal is to resell and profit, and you may need to spend money on repairs, so keep the original cost price as low as possible.

Once you've decided on a website and a color palette, start with tiny cash investments.

Chapter 8

How to Earn Money from Amazon Returns

As previously stated, the purpose of purchasing Amazon returns is to resell them. So, the ideal method to profit from Amazon returns is to use your purchases to launch a retail arbitrage business. The main problem is that not all of the things you receive will be satisfactory;

you may need to fix them before relisting them at a higher price.

Here are two strategies for increasing your chances of profiting from Amazon refunds.

Refurbish and Repair

Spend as much time as possible maintaining and updating the products to maximize their resale value. The key to profiting from consumer returns is to make them look as good as new.

The products in the pallets frequently have missing pieces or misplaced packaging accessories. Replacing missing parts and packaging materials might boost your product's resale value.

Try Product Bundling

Product bundling is an excellent approach for swiftly selling out. The trick is to combine complementary products and sell them as a package at a discount.

You may sell a bag beside a matching shoe. This way, you can swiftly deplete the contents of your pallet and recoup your investment.

Chapter 9

Should You Purchase Amazon Returns?

Yes, if you want to start a retail arbitrage with a little upfront cost, you should consider purchasing Amazon returns. However, there is a substantial level of risk involved, therefore it is not guaranteed to make you money.

However, if you are ready to take the risk, it is a fantastic method to make money online. To get started, you won't need much storage space or any technological knowledge; all you need to do is increase the resale worth of your products.

Reselling is an excellent method to enter the Amazon marketplace; nevertheless, you should carefully consider your alternatives before purchasing Amazon returns.

Printed in Great Britain
by Amazon

32370209R00030